# LUDLOW
## THROUGH TIME
Dorothy Nicolle

First published 2012

Amberley Publishing
The Hill, Stroud
Gloucestershire, GL5 4EP

www.amberley-books.com

Copyright © Dorothy Nicolle, 2012

The right of Dorothy Nicolle to be identified as the
Author of this work has been asserted in accordance
with the Copyrights, Designs and Patents Act 1988.

ISBN 978 1 4456 0847 1

British Library Cataloguing in Publication Data.
A catalogue record for this book is available from
the British Library.

Typeset in 9.5pt on 12pt Celeste.
Typesetting by Amberley Publishing.
Printed in the UK.

# Contents

| | | |
|---|---|---|
| | Acknowledgements | 4 |
| | Introduction | 5 |
| CHAPTER 1 | Ludlow Castle | 7 |
| CHAPTER 2 | The Square | 15 |
| CHAPTER 3 | St Lawrence's Church | 23 |
| CHAPTER 4 | Towards the Bull Ring | 31 |
| CHAPTER 5 | Broad Street | 41 |
| CHAPTER 6 | The Old Town Walls & Beyond | 51 |
| CHAPTER 7 | Into the Suburbs | 63 |
| CHAPTER 8 | Along the River Teme | 73 |
| CHAPTER 9 | Further Afield | 85 |

# Acknowledgements

It is always such fun to find old photographs and then try to recreate the scene or simply to work out where the earlier photographer stood and see how things have changed over the years. I have had so much help in both my search for the old and my discovery of the new. I wish to thank Shropshire Museums for the use of a number of photographs in their collection and particularly, in Ludlow Library, Avril Lines and Howard Cheese for giving up so much of their time. Another special thank you goes to Frank Tipton for the use of many pictures in his own collection. Finally, but by no means least, I wish to thank Stanton Stevens of the Castle Bookshop for introducing me to so many wonderful people.

91171    Ludlow Castle from the

# Introduction

Ludlow is one of those rarities in Britain – a deliberately planned town. Dating back to Norman times its history began with the establishment of a castle in the 1080s, built to control the recently subdued English and also to protect William the Conqueror's western border from incursions by the Welsh.

No sooner had the castle been built than local people gravitated towards it and the relative safety it provided. It didn't take long for their Norman overlords to realise that here was an additional source of income and so a market was established. Markets brought money in a number of ways – not only did they encourage a general increase in business in themselves but traders could be forced not only to attend this (and no other) market but to pay tolls for the privilege of trading there. And Ludlow's market was enormous, stretching as it did all the way from the eastern walls of the castle to the junction of Old Street and Corve Street – a wide, open area; even today it takes some five minutes to walk from one end to the other.

Inevitably, over the centuries, such an open area was too much of a temptation for builders so that before long temporary structures appeared within the market area which were soon replaced by more permanent buildings. This means that today the former market area is criss-crossed with narrow streets which easily become crammed with traffic.

Meanwhile Ludlow began to develop in other ways, too, besides being an important trading centre. Then, in 1485, occurred an event that was to change Ludlow's perception of itself for ever. That event was the Battle of Bosworth Field. It may have taken place many miles away in Leicestershire but, with the accession of Henry Tudor to the throne of England, Ludlow's role changed. No longer was it a border town protecting England from the Welsh. From now on Wales and England were united under one monarch, and Wales needed to be administered.

No-one in London, however, fancied being sent to the wilds of the far west to enforce law and order. Civilisation, so far as the members of Henry's court were concerned, ended at the English borders. And so the administrators and lawyers, politicians and hangers-on came to Ludlow. For the next two hundred or so years Ludlow became, despite the fact that it was in England, the virtual capital of Wales, ruled over by the Lord Lieutenant in the Marches. This was a post created by the King and those who held it controlled the entire region and were answerable only to the monarch.

With the Lord Lieutenant came the Prince of Wales and wherever a prince went a court soon followed. Before long Ludlow had acquired an air of class and nobility which, even now, it still retains. Despite the presence of Shrewsbury, a few miles up the road and the acknowledged county capital, it was Ludlow that had the cachet that drew the local nobility like a magnet.

Even when in the 1700s the town saw a decline in its importance following the removal of the administrators back to London, this association with class and style remained. You have only to walk along Broad Street to see the evidence of this – all those wonderful Georgian buildings grace almost the entire street. The people who built those houses obviously intended to spend a great deal of their time in a town that should, at that point, have been in decline.

Today this association with class and refinement remains. Ludlow is regularly voted as one of the nicest towns in the country in which to live – a fact that keeps house prices here exorbitantly high. It has also now acquired a new reputation for good living. This began in the 1950s with the first Ludlow Festival. Now an annual event that takes over the entire town for almost a month every summer, it draws people from all over the world, particularly to its highlight event – a Shakespeare play performed in the grounds of Ludlow Castle. Then in the 1990s came a new reputation – this time for quality food. At one point restaurants in the little town of Ludlow held more Michelin stars than any other town in the country. This resulted in the establishment of an annual Food Fair which, like the Festival, quickly acquired a name for itself.

Ludlow may be considered by some to be a small backwater country town (its population is only 10,000 after all) but it's got a big, first-class reputation.

# CHAPTER 1

# Ludlow Castle

## Ludlow Castle

We're fortunate today to have any remains of Ludlow Castle at all. In the 1700s a decision was made in the town to demolish the entire structure and sell off the stone. Fortunately a Shropshire architect, Thomas Farnolls Pritchard, was asked to prepare costings for the work. He wanted to save the castle so he deliberately overestimated the cost of demolition and underestimated the value of the stone. The project was deemed to be too expensive and so was abandoned.

### The Gateway to Ludlow Castle

The cannon pictured here is a Russian one that was captured following the Battle of Sebastopol during the Crimean War and subsequently given to the town in 1857. In fact there were dozens of such cannons presented to various towns around the country but most have since disappeared. Apparently, many of them were used for scrap metal during the Second World War. It's the metal from one of these cannons that has since been used to make Victoria Cross medals.

### Ludlow Castle

These days you are much more likely to see a flock of tourists grazing in the outer bailey of Ludlow's castle than a flock of sheep. The castle is privately owned – it was first leased and then purchased in 1811 by the Earl of Powis and it still belongs to the family today.

LUDLOW CASTLE FROM WALK

## The Mortimer Tower

Wherever you walk around the outside of the castle, the ruins are most impressive. They are haunted, too, by Marion de Bruyere. Tricked by her lover into betraying the castle in the late 1200s, Marion is said to have first killed him with his own sword before jumping to her death from the battlements. This legend forms the background to a recent book, *The Smile of a Ghost*, by Phil Rickman, a novel in which the town of Ludlow also plays its part.

### Castle Keep Tower

When the Normans arrived in England in 1066 they promptly set about building castles from where they could subdue and control the recently conquered English. Invariably the first castles were built in a hurry and were made of wood. Ludlow's castle, however, was made of stone from the beginning and the oldest part of it is the keep, which can be seen here rising above and protecting the entrance.

## Castle Banqueting Hall

Can there be a more perfect backdrop for a theatre stage than the banqueting hall of Ludlow Castle? It serves that purpose each year during the month of the Ludlow Festival. Here we see rehearsals for the 2012 production of *Much Ado About Nothing*. Shakespeare's plays are timeless and this was proved once again with this production, which was performed as though the story was taking place in the Second World War.

## Chapel in Ludlow Castle

Believe it or not, this structure is actually the nave of the chapel, the chancel having been demolished long since. Round chapels in this country were often associated with the medieval Knights Templar, who were amongst the finest soldiers fighting in the Crusades, and this was the case with this chapel, which was dedicated to St Mary Magdalene.

CHAPTER 2

# The Square

### The Castle Gardens

It was the wife of the then Earl of Powis who, in the early 1800s, was behind the laying out of the grounds that surrounded the castle as gardens and walkways for the public. This is still a beautiful area to sit and linger. Carefully positioned in the garden is this strange piece. It's by a local blind artist, Seren Thomas – this is art that has to be touched to be enjoyed.

## Castle Lodge

Like so many buildings in Ludlow, Castle Lodge is a fascinating mixture of stone and timber. In Tudor times the building was used as a prison and conditions were so foul that it was described at the time as 'such a place of punishment as the common people termed it a hell'. Today it is privately owned but it is still possible to visit and admire the fine plaster ceilings in the main reception rooms.

### The Square and Old Town Hall

Described by Nikolaus Pevsner as 'Ludlow's bad luck', the Victorian Town Hall pictured on the right was demolished in 1986. The timing was convenient for the producers of the television version of Tom Sharpe's novel, *Blott on the Landscape*, which had been published in 1975. About to be demolished, it was therefore an excellent backdrop for the courthouse scenes in the drama and could be happily wrecked in the process.

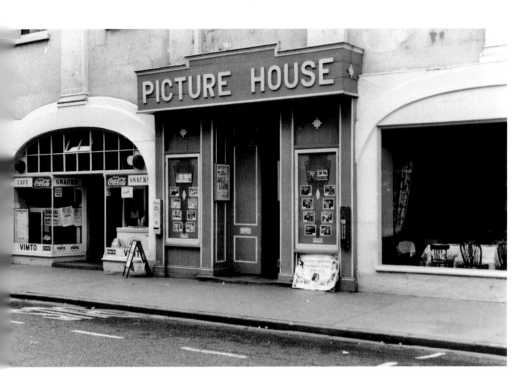

### The Assembly Hall and Museum

This 1960 photograph of what is now the entrance to Ludlow's museum and visitor information centre shows the former cinema with an advertisement for *The Nun's Story* starring Audrey Hepburn. In its heyday in the 1940s and '50s queues of people waiting to see films here would extend for a fair distance down Mill Street around the corner.

*The Market Square, Ludlow*

### The Square and Market

Once the old Town Hall (on the left, above) was demolished it meant that the open area of the Square could once again revert to its former use as a large, open market area. Regular markets are held here throughout the year including, as is the case here, an antiques market usually held on the first Sunday of the month. Pictured here is the back of a second-hand book stall.

## Church Street in 1960

Four separate streets all open up on the eastern side of Ludlow's Square. Only one of the streets is wide enough to allow for vehicles to use it, the others are narrow little alleyways. Church Street, pictured here, is one of them. It's just possible to see in the far distance on the left, the old Town Hall in the Square beyond.

## Church Street – College Street Junction in 1960

I collect pub signs as a hobby – not, I hasten to add, the real thing, but photographs of signs. The building on the right of the 1960 photograph shows a corner of the Church Inn and today it displays what has to be one of my favourite pub signs anywhere. Every time you look at this sign you can see something new.

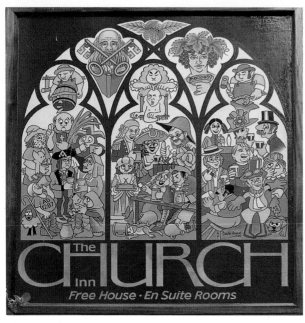

# CHAPTER 3

# St Lawrence's Church

ST LAWRENCE'S CHURCH, LUDLOW

### St Lawrence's Church

At 203 feet long and with a tower that is 135 feet high, St Lawrence's Church is the largest in Shropshire. Indeed it claims, also, to be the largest parish church in England. The tower can easily be seen as you approach Ludlow but once you get into the town it disappears behind a mass of buildings and streets. Notice, in the modern photograph, how all the tombs and tombstones have been removed. I always think this is a pity, even if it does allow for easier maintenance.

Ludlow Church.

**West End of St Lawrence's Church**

*'Loveliest of trees, the cherry now*
*Is hung with bloom along the bough...'*
Just to the right of the west door of
St Lawrence's Church a cherry tree has
now been planted. It commemorates the
poet, A. E. Housman, whose ashes were
buried nearby. Houman's collection of
poems, *A Shropshire Lad,* was published in
1896 and it is said that, after the Bible, it
was the favourite book for soldiers in the
First World War to carry in their pockets
because his words were so evocative of
the countryside back home.

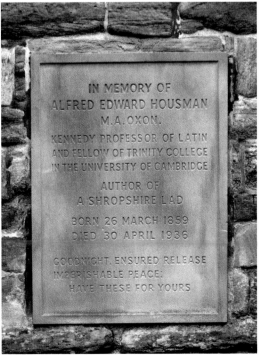

IN MEMORY OF
ALFRED EDWARD HOUSMAN
M.A. OXON.
KENNEDY PROFESSOR OF LATIN
AND FELLOW OF TRINITY COLLEGE
IN THE UNIVERSITY OF CAMBRIDGE

AUTHOR OF
A SHROPSHIRE LAD

BORN 26 MARCH 1859
DIED 30 APRIL 1936

GOODNIGHT. ENSURED RELEASE
IMPERISHABLE PEACE:
HAVE THESE FOR YOURS

### St Lawrence's Church – High Altar

John Ireland writing in the 1500s described St Lawrence's as 'very fayre and large, and richly adorned'. It is when you enter St Lawrence's that you begin to recognise the wealth that was to be found in Ludlow. This wealth came from many sources – in medieval times it was the wool trade that made not just Ludlow but England, too, so wealthy. Then, in Tudor times, money came from the court (both social and legal) that established itself here.

St Lawrence's Church. Ludlow.

### St Lawrence's Church – the Chancel

As Prince of Wales, Prince Arthur, the eldest son of King Henry VII, came to live in Ludlow Castle with his new wife, Catherine of Aragon. Within months of their wedding he died here and his heart lies buried somewhere in the vicinity of the High Altar. The rest of his body, however, was taken to Worcester Cathedral for burial.

ARTHUR
PRINCE OF WALES
DIED AT LUDLOW CASTLE
2nd APRIL 1502
AGED 15 YEARS 7 MONTHS
His Heart was buried near this place

### The Misericords of St Lawrence's Church

A misericord (or mercy seat as it is sometimes known) is a small wooden shelf on the underside of a folding seat, providing a shelf that someone standing for long periods in a church service can rest on. Those in St Lawrence's Church are exquisite. Most of them were carved in the 1400s and many depict scenes of everyday life as with the postcard shot here showing a man (who seems half cut already) pouring himself a drink. My favourite of them all, however, shows a man warming his feet by the fire.

## The Masque of Comus

The origins of the Ludlow Festival go back to 1634 when John Milton's *Comus* was first performed here. Then in the 1950s money was needed in order to restore the roof of St Lawrence's Church and so another performance was staged. It was such a success that, from 1960, the Ludlow Festival became an annual event that now takes over almost the entire town each summer. The modern photograph shows the Festival box office with posters of previous Shakespeare productions on either side of the window.

### The Reader's House

This building, with its wonderful mixture of stone and timber, originally housed the schoolmaster. Today it's a private house so that only that part facing the churchyard can be viewed by the public. The carved front porch, which was added in the early 1600s, is a delight with its carving detail and decorative ironwork on the door.

# CHAPTER 4

# Towards the Bull Ring

THE NARROWS, LUDLOW.

## King Street

Nicknamed the Narrows for obvious reasons, this is actually the beginning of King Street and is always a scene of congestion these days. Notice the gas lamp on the pavement in the old postcard, which dates from the early 1900s.

### The Bull Ring Tavern

With the date 1365 proudly painted over one of its windows and a slight change of name that proclaims it now to be Ye Olde Bull Ring Tavern, the Bull Ring Tavern claims to be the oldest public house in Ludlow. I must admit, however, that I favour the Bull in nearby Corve Street for that accolade, although undoubtedly they have both been offering sustenance and accommodation to the town's visitors for centuries.

## The Bull Ring and the Tolsey

Once known as the Beast Market, this was the part of the old, medieval market that was nearest to the eastern town gates. Little seems to have changed here in the forty or so years since the earlier photograph was taken, just the design of the cars. The bunting in the later picture was put up to celebrate the Queen's Jubilee but also was well timed for the visit to Ludlow of the Olympic Torch, which was brought through the town the day after the photograph was taken.

## The Tolsey

One of the shops in the Tolsey has an odd name – Pye Powder. This was where those coming to trade had to pay their tolls. It was also the site of a Court of *Pied Poudre* or *dusty feet*. In other words it was here that plaintiffs could bring their problems for testing in an acknowledged court of law and get their arguments sorted out when they came into town 'before they even had time to clean the dust off their feet'. The court cases tended to be minor, localised, ones such as boundary disputes between neighbours.

### The Feathers Hotel

'The Welsh are a litigious race and Ludlow did very well out of it.' So said a friend of mine on one occasion and, I wish to add, this friend is Welsh. Consequently it must come as no surprise to learn that the Feathers Hotel was originally built in the early 1600s as the private house of a lawyer – his name was Rhys Jones and his initials are carved into the main doorway.

**'The Feathers Hotel and Posting House; Billiards'**

So reads the sign on the side of the building in this photograph. I like the way that 'billiards' are considered a greater attraction than clean sheets, good food or whatever ales they served inside. The Feathers became an inn (with stabling for 100 horses) in 1670 and is, today, considered one of the finest country town hotels in Britain.

### The Interior of the Feathers Hotel

Formerly a dining room as pictured here, this ornately decorated room is now a private sitting room for the hotel's residents. Rhys Jones obviously had pretensions to grandeur when he used the royal coat of arms in the centre of his elaborately plastered ceiling.

## The Bull Inn, Corve Street

Appearances can be so deceptive. Looking at these buildings from the street you would assume the timber building beyond the pub is the older. Instead the Bull predates it by centuries. The Bull is also reputed to be haunted by a sixteenth-century priest who took refuge there. Interestingly, when doing renovations in the building not so long ago a priest's hole was found near the old fireplace.

**The Courtyard of the Bull Inn in the 1950s**
It is when you enter the courtyard that you realise how old this building is. And it seems there are no new ideas in this world. The Bull, in fact, was a medieval version of a motel, with stabling for the horses on the ground floor and rooms (or, more likely, shared beds) for the guests above. In recent years the Bull has gained a reputation for the jazz and blues concerts that are held in the courtyard during the Ludlow Festival.

CHAPTER 5

# Broad Street

### King Street and the Buttercross

Notice how, in the old photograph, the two cars on the right are parked facing each other. These days, however, traffic is such that the street has now been made one way. Even that hasn't stopped problems caused by the timber building on the left and the way it overhangs into the street so that high vehicles and coaches need to take a wide curve as they pass by. But they still keep bumping into it.

### The Buttercross

The Buttercross has had a chequered history. The upper floor was used at first to house a Blue Coat School. These were charitable schools founded in the 1700s. They were so-called because each pupil was given, each year, a coat to wear and blue was the cheapest dye at the time. In the 1950s it became, for a time, a museum, described as one of the best small town museums in the country.

## The View from the Buttercross in the 1920s/'30s

The Buttercross building cost £1,000 when it was built in the 1740s. This view looks down Broad Street from the Buttercross at the top. The ground floor area has always been used as a market selling, not surprisingly, butter in the past. It is still regularly used by traders to this day.

BROAD STREET AND BUTTER CROSS, LUDLOW.

### The Buttercross and Bodenhams

This somewhat idealised picture postcard from the 1950s or '60s picks out the detail of the timber buildings on the right. The building at the top of the street was built in the early 1400s by the Palmer's Guild in what would probably then have been virtually the middle of the market place. The Palmer's Guild, however, was so powerful and wealthy that, even had there been planning restrictions at the time, they would have simply ignored them. Today it is home to Bodenhams, a family-run clothing business.

**De Grey's Café in Broad Street**
Formerly a pub called The Swan, De Grey's opened as a teashop in the 1920s and soon gained a reputation as 'one of the larger and finer café-restaurants in the Midlands'. It still serves tea and cakes, along with larger meals for those who want them. The waitresses still dress in black and white, much as they would have done when it first opened.

## The Angel Hotel

This odd-looking building served as an inn for over 400 years which must be some kind of a record. Perhaps the most famous people to stay here were Admiral Lord Nelson who came here in 1802 to receive the Freedom of the Borough and was accompanied by both his mistress Emma, and her husband Lord Hamilton! Today, however, the building has been converted into apartments.

## Broad Street

It's interesting to note how much more uniform, not to say bland, Broad Street looked one hundred years ago when so many of the buildings, regardless of how they had been built, were covered with plaster. Now, with timber or brick revealed there is an exuberance about the façades that cannot help but please. No wonder Nikolaus Pevsner described Broad Street as 'one of the most memorable streets in England'.

*Broad Street, Ludlow.*

### Broad Street and Lloyds Bank
Enlargement of the old photograph reveals a carving above the entrance to the building on the right that is still there today. That black horse symbol that we associate with Lloyds Bank was only adopted in the late 1800s. Before that it was a beehive, representing 'thrift and industry', that was the symbol of the bank. Obviously then, this branch has been here for some time.

### Raven Lane

Not many people who admire the buildings in Broad Street make the effort to look behind. When those grand houses were first built access was required at the rear of the properties for the servants and horses. These days the former mews serving the large mansions have developed to become individual properties in their own right and many, like the one pictured here, have been restored.

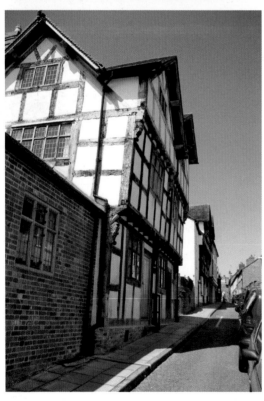

CHAPTER 6

# The Old Town Walls
# & Beyond

## The Broad Gate

What a misnomer the name Broad Gate is for such a narrow entrance. What particularly fascinates me about the rear of this building is the range of different styles of windows in a single wall. With their increasingly large panes of glass and narrowing glazing bars, each of them is representative of the time in which it was inserted.

*The Gate House, Ludlow.*

### The Broad Gate and Wheatsheaf Inn

Ladies, beware if you enter the Wheatsheaf Inn. Apparently it is haunted by a mischievous ghost who delights in pinching the bottoms of those ladies who catch his fancy. There are a number of small, but intriguing, differences in these two pictures – windows in the medieval gatehouse have been altered and there is one addition. Also note that the castellated turret on the left has been removed. The vehicles have changed, too.

## Lower Broad Street

Notice the different levels of the street – this was done by the engineer, Thomas Telford, in order to make the angle of the slope that much easier for horses pulling stagecoaches up and down the hill. In the early 1800s when this was done Ludlow was a major coaching centre with nearly thirty mail coaches alone racing through the town each week, linking Ludlow with London, Bristol, Chester and towns all over the country.

## Lower Broad Street

Today the different levels between the main road and the pavement provide a wonderful backdrop for householders for their displays of potted plants and flower boxes. Once again, as in Broad Street further up, the building on the right has had its plaster removed to reveal the timber work below, thus nicely breaking up the uniformity of the brick buildings that line the street beside it.

### Corve Street

Goldings Stores Ltd has now become an antiques shop near the top of Corve Street. Judging by the window display when the earlier photograph was taken in 1960, however, some of the prams that were being sold then could easily be considered as potential antiques if they were put on sale in the same shop now.

**The Post Office in Corve Street in 1960**
The former post office building seems to have hardly changed in outward appearance at all. However, its purpose has certainly changed – it now serves as a restaurant with a most appropriate name. It's called The Mail Room.

### Corve Street in 1960

The company of Morris, Barker & Poole, the Ludlow office of which is pictured here in 1960, has now disappeared, having been merged with McCartneys and Tesco has taken over the site. Tesco arrived in Ludlow, to much disapproval from the local townsfolk, in 2000. The unusual (for a modern supermarket) flowing design of the store was a deliberate attempt to ensure that it fitted in with the other eighteenth- and nineteenth-century buildings that line Corve Street.

*Lane's Asylum, Ludlow*

*A HAPPY CHRISTMAS*

## Old Street and Lane's Asylum

Today when we talk of an asylum we automatically tend to think of a madhouse. However, this is not necessarily the case – to give someone asylum is to give them refuge. And so it was with the building here. Mind you it also served as a workhouse and so I'm not sure just how comfortable such an asylum would have been for those who needed it. It is now a private house.

## The Junction of Lower and Upper Galdeford

This rather fuzzy photograph probably dates from around the turn of the nineteenth and twentieth centuries. Notice the gas lamp on the left with, just beside it, a gentleman standing with his hand in his pocket, displaying the fob watch he wears on his waistcoat. Incidentally, Galdeford is pronounced 'jailford' – something that had me confused for years.

### The Junction of Lower and Upper Galdeford

A slightly different view of the same road junction. The Portcullis pub across the road disappeared to make way for the Co-op and the car park entrance. The word portcullis means a sliding door or gate and, of course, these were usually found at the main entrance to a castle. Here, the pub's name probably derived from the fact that it stood near to the site of the east gate of the medieval town.

### Demolition of Tannery Buildings, Lower Galdeford

I love the fact that there's not a hard hat in sight in this early photograph – so much for health and safety issues. Notice how one man stands perched on the half-demolished wall of the former house. Although it at first appears as though just the one house is being taken down, if you look beyond you can see that another house further along the street has also already lost its roof.

CHAPTER 7

# Into the Suburbs

### The Roman Catholic Church

Described once as looking 'like an art deco priest's house', St Peter's Church was built in 1936 by the Italian-Welsh architect, Giuseppe Rinvolucri. Notice the upside-down crosses on the gate – St Peter is said to have been crucified in the time of the Emperor Nero and asked that his cross should be that way because he considered himself to be unworthy to be crucified in the same way as Jesus.

Amongst the memorials inside the church is one dedicated to Bertram 'Jimmy' James, one of the few survivors of the Great Escape from Stalag Luft III in 1944. He died in 2008, aged ninety-two.

### The Raven Pub

Like so many pubs up and down the country the Raven could not compete with supermarket prices for its beer. The pub was demolished in 2007, having closed a few years previously. And guess what? It has now been replaced by a supermarket.

### Livesey Road

Despite the suburban look of the houses on the left, this picture has almost a rural feel about it. Not any more though, with tarmac and lines painted along the road. At the far end of the street there's a holy well that (miraculously?) is still there today, sitting in the middle of the road, which, for a few yards, becomes a dual carriageway at that point.

### St Mary's Lane

The reference point for these two photographs is the timber building in Corve Street beyond. The early photograph dates from the 1960s when the gateway on the left led into Pipe's Farm – a working farm despite the fact that it was in the town suburbs. Notice the cow's muck in the street in front of the gate.

### Sheet Road

The building pictured here was a former turnpike cottage that, unfortunately, was destroyed in 1980, so that today the only point of reference is the building behind it. Sheet Road, on the eastern boundary of Ludlow, saw a great deal of development in the 1990s with the establishment of an industrial park serving the town – the red van pictured is driving into the industrial park area.

### The Bell House in Ludford

This beautiful building dates from 1614. It served as an inn, the Old Bell, for many years, hence its present name. Now a private house, it's no surprise that the wooden fence has been replaced by a hedge, which has been allowed to grow quite high. Consequently, I've taken the modern photograph from the churchyard overlooking Ludford.

## The Old Mill at Ludford

Just because Ludlow developed into an administrative and social centre does not mean that there was no industry here. In fact there were several mills established along the banks of the River Teme, some of which have survived to be converted into private homes. This one was formerly a fulling mill where woollen cloth was cleaned and beaten. The heavy rains in the summer of 2012 meant that the river pictured here is in full spate and the noise from the weir is thunderous.

## Ludford Lodge Youth Hostel

Once again we have a building that, in this case, has now reverted back to its former role as a private house. Many of the youth hostellers who came here would have chosen Ludlow as a base for walking holidays in the hills of southern Shropshire. Indeed, my own father first came to the town when in his teens in the 1930s for just such a holiday.

## A Plethora of Chimneys

The pub sitting on the south bank of Ludford Bridge is the Charlton Arms. The Charlton family were great local landowners. One member of the family was Sir Job Charlton, one time speaker of the House of Commons in the seventeenth century. His tomb in the church has a painted effigy lying on the top and the artist has copied this when painting the pub sign. Notice also the massive chimneys on the building beyond; there are two great banks of them, one on either side of the pair of semi-detached houses.

CHAPTER 8

# Along the River Teme

LUDFORD BRIDGE, LUDLOW.

### Ludford Bridge

The present Ludford Bridge, heading towards Herefordshire, dates from the fifteenth century although there would certainly have been an earlier one on the site. It's a narrow bridge with two passing places on each side but these have never been large enough for modern vehicles. Consequently, the first set of traffic lights to be erected in southern Shropshire were set up to control the traffic crossing this bridge.

*·dlow. River Teme.*      *Weir and Mills from Ludford Bridge.*

### The Horseshoe Weir

Before any bridge was built people would still have needed to get across the river somehow. In fact there was fording point across the Teme at just about the point where this weir now sits. That river crossing had been important long before there was ever a town here – Old Street in Ludlow is so named because it was an old routeway, possibly a prehistoric route, that led down to this ford.

### The River Teme

The name 'Teme' has a curious history – it may well derive from an ancient prehistoric Celtic word, *Tamesa*, meaning the dark one. It has given rise to several river names in Britain such as the Thames, Thame and the Tamar to mention just a few. In 1996 the whole length of this river was designated as an SSSI (Site of Special Scientific Interest) by English Nature. At 81 miles in length it's the sixteenth longest river in the UK.

### Ludford Bridge from Upstream

The vegetation all along the river banks means that it's absolutely impossible these days to see the Ludford Bridge as you walk along the footpaths beside the River Teme. It's interesting to note how low the water level is in the earlier of these photographs – it must have been taken during a dry summer. In normal circumstances the weirs all along the river as it wends around Ludlow keep river levels much higher than this.

### The River Teme

The River Teme is normally a fast-flowing river which, in medieval times, would have been excellent for providing power. But such power needs to be controlled and so four weirs were built along this stretch of river to ensure that the power was as constant as possible for the many mills that were then erected on the river banks. Many of the mills were corn mills but others were used for fulling – fulling was a process in the production of woollen cloth in which the newly woven cloth was washed and pounded to eliminate any oils, dirt or impurities in the wool.

General View, Ludlow.

## Mill Street and the Weir Upstream of Ludford Bridge

Yes, it is lovely to see so much lush woodland so close to the town providing delightful walking routes. There are times, however, when one feels that a little judicious tree-lopping would be highly beneficial if only to enable those walkers to enjoy the views along the way. This early view of Mill Street from the south bank of the Teme is now almost entirely obliterated.

## The Bread Walk

The mid-1800s saw a period of high unemployment and rising distress among many of the poorer local people. One project that was carried out in order to give employment was the building of a walk route on the southern bank of the Teme. It's now known as the Bread Walk because local tradition has it that the people who worked on the footpath were paid in bread – ostensibly to prevent them from squandering any cash they earned in the local alehouses.

## Dinham Bridge

In the 1800s this bridge was known as the New Bridge as it was only built in 1823. However, that's not to say it was totally new – it replaced a bridge that was already here. We don't know, though, when the earliest bridge was built at this position but it seems likely that there would have been a bridge here from soon after the time the castle above was built, if only to control the main route westwards towards Wales.

**Dinham Bridge and Castle**

The footpath sign in the foreground marks the beginning of the Mortimer Trail, which was opened in 2002. The trail is thirty miles long and goes from Ludlow to Kington. It is so-called because it meanders through lands that were once under the control of the powerful Mortimer family. Indeed, Ludlow Castle and castles at nearby Wigmore and Cleobury were also owned by the Mortimers.

### Ludlow Castle from Meadows

The castle's wonderfully commanding position is evident from the playing fields by the river. Today, although football is often still played here, there is a much wider variety of apparatus available and it regularly draws young families at the weekend. Notice the newly-planted willow tree – several have been planted along the river banks in the hope that these thirsty plants will help lessen the impact of flooding in the area.

### Ludlow from Whitcliffe

Today the finest viewpoint over Ludlow has to be that from Whitcliffe Common. The common is around 52 acres in size, a fraction of what it would have been in medieval times when the burgesses of the town could not just graze their livestock here but also collect firewood and hay from the site and even quarry stone to build their homes. These days the area is carefully managed to preserve the variety of the flora, with the grass only being cut once a year, after the flowering plants have had a chance to seed.

# CHAPTER 9

# Further Afield

### Stanton Lacy – the Church

The settlement at Stanton was here long before there was anything at Ludlow and this wonderful old church is a reminder of that long history. In fact Ludlow was originally in the parish of Stanton. Parts of the church date back to pre-Norman times and, inevitably with a building of that age, it needs constant maintenance and costly repairs. Fortunately, work is being done but there is a current appeal for help to finance the work.

STANTON LACY POST OFFICE

## Stanton Lacy – the Old Post Office

The village of Stanton Lacy once had, besides its church, two schools, four chapels, shops, pubs and even a football team. And, as you can see, the former post office, too, has now gone. It is difficult, at first, to realise that this is one and the same building, it looks so different. Mind you, the letter box in front of the house reminds us of its former role as a post office.

Bromfield. Post Office &c.

### Bromfield – a General View

Little has changed with the buildings in the old photograph and so I chose, instead, to picture a new building just beyond. It's the prestigious Ludlow Food Centre. With the establishment of a foodie reputation for the town in the 1990s it was inevitable that such a centre should evolve and it opened in 2007. Not only is it a farm shop selling local products but it also has several kitchens producing bread, pies, jams, pickles ... in fact over 50 per cent of the prepared foods sold are also produced here.

## Bromfield – the Priory Gatehouse

The differences between these two photographs come about because the early shot shows the rear of the gatehouse, seen from the churchyard beyond, and my photograph shows the front. As its name suggests this was the gatehouse to a medieval priory that has long gone. Today, it is in the care of the Landmark Trust, an organisation that rescues historic buildings and converts them into holiday accommodation, in this case for up to six people.

## Stokesay Castle

Despite its name, Stokesay Castle (pictured also on page 85) is not a castle at all and never was. Look at those large windows overlooking a narrow moat – there could be nothing defensive about them. Instead it is what is known as a medieval moated manor house. It was built in the late 1200s by a wealthy wool merchant named Lawrence de Ludlow. Today it is one of the jewels in the English Heritage crown.

The Gate House

### Stokesay Castle Gatehouse

Stokesay Castle was slighted (in other words partially destroyed) in the Civil War so that the gatehouse, pictured here, was then rebuilt. Like so many timber buildings of the period it is covered with decoration but my favourite carving is easily that of the green man carved into the wood on the corner of the building – it is just possible to make him out in the early photograph.

### Craven Arms Hotel

Craven Arms is one of those rare places that is actually named after an inn rather than the other way around. It was the arrival of the railways which made this place develop and it was then that it got its name, from the inn pictured here. Notice the pillar, partially obscured by trees, in the modern picture. This is a milestone giving such essential information as the fact that Edinburgh is 205 miles away – just what you need to know as you cycle around Shropshire.

HOTEL & SCHOOLS, CRAVEN ARMS

### Stokesay Castle Hotel, Craven Arms

The Stokesay Castle Hotel has now become simply the Stokesay Inn but otherwise, externally at least, appears unaltered. Beyond it, then and now, is the town's primary school, also known as the Stokesay Primary School. This all may seem strange at first until you remember that the name Craven Arms is relatively modern and for all but the last hundred or so years, this town was within the parish of Stokesay.

## Clee Hill

Looking at the early photograph here I always feel that it could be a scene in some town in the American Wild West and, indeed, one does feel that one is entering wild country when approaching it. Clee Hill is one of the highest settlements in Shropshire, sitting on the side of Titterstone Clee with magnificent views to the south, but it is often totally cut off by winter snows.

## The Arbor Tree at Aston-on-Clun

It was a tradition in pagan times to decorate trees in winter time in order to encourage them to come into leaf in the spring. Time passed and the tradition died out (except when we decorate Christmas trees). Then it was revived in 1660 when many oak trees were decorated to celebrate the accession to the throne of Charles II who had hidden in such a tree after the Battle of Worcester. Once again the tradition died but, here in Aston-on-Clun, it has survived and this tree is adorned with flags each year.

## Heath Chapel

Heath Chapel, up in the Clee Hills and miles from anywhere, has to be one of my favourite churches in all of Shropshire, so I make no excuses for including it in this book. In nearly 1,000 years the structure has not changed at all – except possibly for the swopping of a thatched roof for the present slate one.